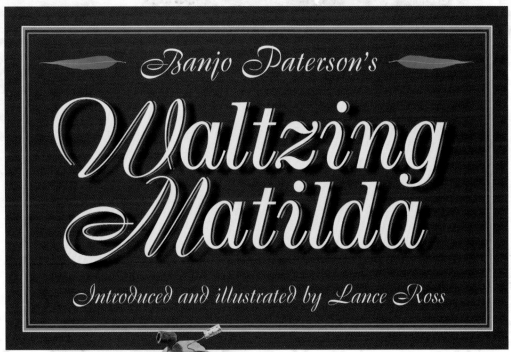

Banjo Paterson's
Waltzing Matilda

Introduced and illustrated by Lance Ross

The Five Mile Press

Pictorial Acknowledgements

The Author and Publisher thank H. A. & C. Glad for permission to reproduce the humorous illustrations by Norman Lindsay; the National Gallery of Victoria, Melbourne and the Art Gallery of Western Australia, Perth, for permission to reproduce images from their galleries; and the Reserve Bank of Australia for permission to reproduce a ten dollar note.

The Five Mile Press

The Five Mile Press Pty Ltd
950 Stud Road
Rowville Victoria 3178 Australia

Phone: + 61 3 8756 5500
Email: publishing@fivemile.com.au

First published 2004

Concept, text, colour illustrations © Lance Ross
Song lyrics by A.B. 'Banjo' Paterson
Music by Marie Cowan
Pen drawings © Norman Lindsay

Designed by Sylvia Witte
Cover design by Lance Ross
Printed in Hong Kong

National Library of Australia Cataloguing in Publication data
Ross, Lance.
Banjo Paterson's Waltzing Matilda

ISBN 1 74124 184 7.

1.Waltzing Matilda (song). 2. National songs – Australia. 3. Folk songs – Australia. 4. Australia – Social life and customs. I. Paterson, A.B. (Andrew Barton), 1864–1941. II. Lindsay, Norman, 1879 – 1969. III. Cowan, Marie. IV. Title

A821. 2

Contents

Foreword

Australia's rich heritage goes back to the 'Dreamtime', the period of thousands of years when the Aborigines were the sole inhabitants of this vast sleeping continent. After European settlement as a penal colony in 1788, explorers such as Bass and Flinders mapped the coastline, and Burke and Wills, Hume and Hovell, and many others, discovered what lay inland. Australians established a democratic nation with federation in 1901. The Anzac tradition, forged at Gallipoli, has come to represent Aussie grit and determination.

Over the decades, there have been plenty of larrikins, good sports, mates and heroes – including some great political leaders, artists, writers, poets, sporting champions, and even an outlaw. This is, of course, Ned Kelly, who became a national icon for showing the fighting spirit with which Australians identify. 'Give him a fair go' is an integral part of the Australian ethos. This refusal simply to accept abuse of power has played a strong role in our history. It was exemplified during the Eureka Stockade uprising and continues to appear in Australian everyday life.

The notion of the 'fair go' explains in part the fame and appeal of the swagman in Banjo Paterson's 'Waltzing Matilda'. He 'nicks' ('poaches' seems too strong a word here) a sheep to survive in the bush.

When the jig is up, he drowns himself rather than be caught, and face the severe punishments of the day – 'You'll never catch me alive!' says he. And so the empathy and sympathy is built into what has become a much loved and embellished Australian character – the swaggie.

I love Australia. I love the bush and the fact that I can wander freely through it without the fear of being eaten. Many of us probably feel that, under different circumstances, we might have been swaggies.

I hope you like this book. I loved creating it. Two of my art heroes are the American artist Norman Rockwell, famed for his front covers of *Saturday Evening Post* magazine, every one of which related in some way to human behaviour; and Australia's Norman Lindsay for his genius in figure drawing and painting. Many of Lindsay's humorous illustrations are included here.

I am grateful to Captain Ian Murray, OBE, for posing as the swagman portrayed in the illustrations and to John Merry, Sally Edwards, Andrew Stout, Professor Marilyn Fleer and Rowan and Freya Fleer-Stout for posing as the family.

Lance Ross

The Australian swagman

They were a varied lot, these men of the open road. There were hard working shearers travelling from shed to shed on sheep stations all over the country; ne'er-do-wells who had been driven to scrounging by lack of work, broken marriages or just bad luck; businessmen ruined by depression; some who chose not to accept support from the government; wandering bush types who enjoyed the freedom of the outback and its hard-working, easygoing farming and country town folk.

I saw my last swagman camping under Burke Road bridge in North Balwyn, Melbourne, in 1957. I had seen my first on a country road in 1947 – not a rare sight then. But swaggies were most common between the late 19th century and the late 1930s. They trod the tracks all over Australia and even as far off as New Zealand, seeking work and surviving from day to day.

Their bed for the night was a swag, also called a shiralee, drum or bluey. Their kitchen was a billy and a pocket-knife. As well as being used for cooking and tea-making, the billy was their waterproof container where they kept flour for making damper and dry grass to start a fire in the rain. Companionship sometimes stretched to a dog, but the downside was that this meant an extra mouth to feed. However, Fido could also act as a food-gatherer – thanks to Thomas Austin, who in 1859 imported from England and released in Winchelsea, Victoria, 24 rabbits. By 1880 their multitudinous descendants had picked

Storage space for tall stories and yarns to spin

Pipe, sometimes filled with cigarette butts

Cigarette butts

Corks to keep flies at bay. Some wore a fly-net

Usually unshaven and sometimes a bit smelly

Swag: a roll of blankets with gear stored inside

Often ill-fitting, second-hand, worn clothes

Billy-can for boiling water for tea and for cooking. Also waterproof storage for flour and dry grass

Tucker bag for food, utensils, personal items

Rabbit trap for free food, rabbit skins to sell

A dog provided company, warmth and caught rabbits

Bowyangs kept trousers out of dust and mud and prevented spiders and grasshoppers reaching tender areas

Free transport to freedom, tucker and occasional employment. Usually with holes in the sole

almost a million hectares of grassland clean. Swaggies often carried rabbit-skin stretchers – hooped lengths of fencing wire – to dry out the skins, which they sold to furriers and milliners. Possums, foxes, snakes and ducks were also good tucker and easy pickings for swaggies and their dogs. Some swagmen fished, and sold Murray cod to hotels.

Swaggies were said to be 'leading the waterbag' – carrying their waterbag on a stick or, more commonly, 'waltzing Matilda'.

Down on his luck, 1889,
Frederick McCubbin, 1855–1917
Oil on canvas, 145.0 x 183.3 x 14.0 cm
Collection: Art Gallery of Western Australia

This term has a long history, originating in Germany, from where many settlers came, especially to the Barossa Valley wine-making region. The German *auf der Walz* (or *Walze*) means 'on the tramp', while *Mathilde* meant 'female travelling companion'. Until about 1911, young apprentices were sent out on the road to look for work and gain experience. They took blankets, greatcoats or swags to keep them warm at night. Thus it was said that they were 'waltzing Matilda' – their swag was their companion. Other terms were 'humping a bluey' and 'humping drum'.

Australian swaggies travelled by 'padding the hoof' (walking), 'jumping the rattler' (sneaking aboard a train) or hitching a ride on a farmer's bullock dray or horse-drawn or motor lorry. The better off swaggies rode bicycles. Some managed a ride on the steamboats up the Murray–Darling river system to the shearing districts. In 1901, there were about 1.6 million horses in Australia drawing all kinds of vehicles and being ridden by all and sundry, including the military. The resulting manure was certainly useful when gathered for home and commercial gardens, but it attracted massive swarms of flies. The inimitable Australian hat with dangling corks was the ingenious solution to this insect problem – and an essential fashion item for the swaggie.

Back then Australians were heavy smokers, consuming an average of 1.3 kg of tobacco each every year – more than twice the average of 0.6 kg in the UK. And the pipe was another vital part of the swaggie's kit.

They had little choice but to wear the same clothes day after day and, since there are not many laundries available under gum trees, their body odour didn't help them to be invited in for tea by cow cockies or their wives. However, this personal hygiene problem had an upside. It was common for a farmhouse to be encircled by a fence designed to keep the rabbits out of the garden, and the dogs in. To outwit the dogs, the swaggie would lay out his swag and topcoat just outside the gate. Then he would let the dogs out to sniff them while he nipped in through the gate, quickly closing it after him. If he was lucky, he was given a little flour, and a chunk of mutton. A real treat was 'cocky's joy' – golden syrup – which cost one-tenth as much as jam. Sometimes, after doing a job and bathing, he might even receive some eggs, milk and vegetables.

Swaggies' shoes were often lined with card-board when the soles wore through. 'Bowyangs' were tied around their knees to prevent insects and mice (there were occasional mice plagues) from running up and to keep their trousers from dragging in the dust. The life of dinky-di swaggies was not so comfortable but at least they had fresh air and the freedom of the bush.

Sad stories came from families wandering and looking for work. One swaggie's two-year-old son died from the cold. He carried the body 15 kilometres to a police station. Families with half a dozen children pushing wheelbarrows or prams were a common sight. Police stations sometimes gave out food. Some swagmen managed things so they received free tucker but avoided work. They were known as 'sundowners' – they arrived at dusk just in time for supper and left at dawn.

A. B. Paterson's famous song 'Waltzing Matilda, was inspired by two Queensland suicides that came to his attention when he was staying on a Queensland sheep station – one of the men being a member of the shearers' union and the other a swagman. Not many people know the names of the two unfortunate men today. But the song their deaths inspired lives on, and is recognised worldwide as a symbol of Australia.

Falling on hard times

In 1905, Victoria was the only state with the age pension. Commonwealth age and invalid pensions were not introduced until 1909 and 1910. Before then, many of the long-term unemployed had little choice but to become swagmen.

It wasn't only the pioneers and Anzacs who helped to build our nation. Most ordinary folk worked harder than many of us are aware. Even before the Great Depression, many Australians faced great hardship.

Good times came to Australia, and particularly to Victoria, in 1851 with the gold discoveries at Ballarat and Bendigo, which were among the richest alluvial gold deposits in the world. From 1883 to 1888, more gold, silver, lead and opals were found. When Broken Hill Proprietary Company declared a profit of £100,000 in 1886, the rush after precious metals was on again. Melbourne was then one of the richest cities in the world. But the good times were not to last.

The increase in building, railway and pastoral investments happened too quickly. In Melbourne, there was an unsustainable boom in land prices. By the late 1880s, 3 million Australian colonists owed £150 million to British banks, which resulted in British investors panicking and withdrawing funds. In 1890 some Melbourne banks closed their doors. Two years later a run started on the Savings Bank of New South Wales and, for two days, a crowd of frenzied investors attempted to recover their money. Recession, then depression, followed.

The 1890s, which saw the birth of the Australian Labor Party, was destined to be a distressing decade for Australians, with the great maritime strike and (relevant to 'Waltzing Matilda') the shearers' strikes from 1890 to 1894.

Above: UPS AND DOWNS. The bark hut of a young squatter and his wife. At the age of 35, he owned 25,000 sheep, an orchard of 500 trees and had a family of five children. By the time he was 71 his wife and children were all dead and drought caused foreclosure on his property, forcing him to live on the pension.

Left: For those thrown out, their new 'homes' were shanties built on Sydney's sand dunes from rotting timber and hessian bags coated with lime and dripping.

Many unemployed men left the city, choosing the life of a swagman and walking the countryside looking for odd jobs.

single men or 1 shilling and six pence (1s 6d) if they lived with a family. A married man with wife and one child received 8s 6d a week – at a time when a pound of butter cost two shillings and eggs were 1s 6d a dozen. So dripping scrounged from the butcher and spread on bread was often all there was to eat.

Tenants evicted by landlords put together humpies on racecourses, in parks, on sand dunes and in the caves of the Sydney Domain. In 1931, about 350 homeless men, women and children lived in tents and huts at La Perouse beside Sydney's Botany Bay.

It was no wonder that so many men packed their swag and took off into the pristine but testing bush, looking to do odd jobs and sleep under the stars with their campfire, billy, a rabbit or two and, occasionally, a mate to spin a yarn with.

The Australian economy began to recover in 1934.

Wool and wheat prices dropped alarmingly, so farmers earned less for their produce and had less money to spend. Shops closed, farms were abandoned, rents went unpaid, tenants were evicted and debts mounted. There was a sense of despair as unemployment rose sharply. In 1894, severe drought contributed to the downturn. In those days, agricultural produce played a more important role in the economy.

In 1929 the American stock market crashed. Businesses collapsed, thousands of businessmen and investors were ruined. Many of them committed suicide. This was the Great Depression, which spread to Europe and South America as well as Australia. The depression led to widespread poverty and massive unemployment.

Wages declined for those who still had jobs. Men and women searched gutters, bins and rubbish tips for food. Fights broke out over food scraps. The Army dyed surplus khaki greatcoats black and issued them to charities. When a Sydney firm advertised a watchman's job, 500 men applied. People ate boiled wheat, offal, rodents and whatever they could lay their hands on. Although 'soliciting for alms' was illegal, begging was rife. Fleas, flies and rats worsened the plight of the growing numbers living in the slums.

The dole or 'susso' – more genteelly known as 'sustenance payment' – was 5 shillings a week for

'Jumping the rattler' ... This meant a free train ride, but it could result in imprisonment – or even sudden death under the wheels, for those who lost their grip

A.B. ('Banjo') Paterson

Millions of Australians regularly see Banjo Paterson's portrait on the ten-dollar note. Many cultural and sporting events, such as Australian Rules grand finals, begin with the singing of 'Waltzing Matilda'. It was a highlight of the opening ceremony of the Sydney 2000 Olympics, together with a band of galloping bush horsemen, reminiscent of another great Paterson verse, 'The Man from Snowy River'. 'Waltzing Matilda' is sung by Aussies gathered around campfires, children in schools and soldiers serving overseas. It's our song.

Andrew Barton Paterson – it's a name befitting a lawyer, which is just what he was. But when he took to his main love, writing about the Australian bush and its people, he adopted the pseudonym 'The Banjo', after a country racehorse. When his work began to appear in *The Bulletin*, the popular journal of the time, 'The Banjo' soon became a household name. Other famous writers for *The Bulletin* included Henry Lawson and 'Breaker' Morant, while Norman Lindsay and George Lambert were among the journal's gifted artists.

Paterson had a positive attitude towards life and the bush. What he found uplifting, Lawson appeared to find depressing. The two were the most popular writers for *The Bulletin* and, at Lawson's suggestion, they played out a congenial, mock-feud in verse about the pros and cons of bush life. While Henry wrote about '*strings of muddy waterholes ... everlasting flies ... no horizon*' and '*Nothing but the sameness of the ragged, stunted trees,*' Banjo wrote, '*Did you chance to hear a chorus in the shearers' huts at night? ... Did you hear no sweeter voices in the music of the bush? ... Did the magpies rouse your slumbers with their carol sweet and strange? Did you hear the silver chiming of the bell-birds on the range?*'

Pertinent to our story of the swagman, Banjo wrote:

*And it takes him back in fancy, half in laughter,
   half in tears,
To a sound of other voices and a thought of other
   years,
When the wool shed rang with bustle
   from the dawning of the day,
And the shear blades were a-clicking
   to the cry of 'wool away!'*

The Australian ten-dollar note, designed by Max Robinson, features Banjo Paterson, 'Waltzing Matilda' and 'The Man from Snowy River'.

Today, with a population of nearly 20 million, Australian authors are doing well if they sell 10,000 copies of a book. Back in Banjo's time, when our population was only around 4 million, his book *The Man from Snowy River and Other Verses* sold over 100,000 copies! And he had larger sales outside Australia than any other Australian writer.

With public broadcasting not starting until the 1920s (and television not until 1956) the printed word was the people's entertainment – and Paterson was a king of storytellers.

When he was up Kosciusko way in the summer of 1889–90 at 26 years of age, he heard a station stockrider named Jack Riley spin a yarn about 'a colt that got away' which had been 'rounded up by a piece of fearless riding and superb horse-manship'.

The poem Paterson wrote on hearing the yarn glorified the horse-riding skills of the Australian bushman. Along with 'Waltzing Matilda', it is Australia's most famous verse. Most of us are familiar with the words of 'Waltzing Matilda'. But in the past people knew many of Banjo's poems by heart. I once visited a farm with friends and the great-uncle of one of them, sitting there in his black greatcoat, 'gave us' some poems. He began:

There was movement at the station,
  for the word had passed around
That the colt from old Regret had got away,
And had joined the wild bush horses
  – he was worth a thousand pound,
So all the cracks had gathered to the fray.

It was, of course, 'The Man from Snowy River'.

Without missing a word, he continued on to the end of the 104 lines, concluding with:

And down by Kosciusko, where the pine clad ridges raise

Their torn and rugged battlements on high,
Where the air is clear as crystal,
  and the white stars fairly blaze,
At midnight in the cold and frosty sky,
And where around the Overflow
  the reed-beds sweep and sway
To the breezes, and the rolling plains are wide,
The Man from Snowy River is a household word today,
And the stockmen tell the story of his ride.

He then recited 'Clancy of the Overflow' and a couple of other poems. It was quite an experience sitting around the log fire, eating scones and jam and cream, in an antique cottage, with this grand old man conjuring up the past. And all the words live on.

Paterson's other popular poems include 'A Bush Christening', 'The Man from Iron Bark', 'How the Favourite Beat Us' and 'The Geebung Polo Club'. As well as verse, he published a novel, short stories and songs. *The Collected Verse of A.B. Paterson*, published in 1921, has been reprinted many times.

Born in 1864 at Narrambla station, near Orange, New South Wales, and raised in the country, he attended school in Sydney and then studied law at university. Andrew Paterson, the son of a Scottish immigrant grazier, practised as a solicitor until 1900. He was interested in politics and considered standing for parliament. In 1889 he published a political pamphlet condemning the drift of country people to the cities, for which he blamed the ruthlessness of squatters and speculators. He was a member of the world's first ski club at Kiandra near Mt Kosciusko. And, only a few years after cars appeared in Australia, he took part in the Sydney to Melbourne Dunlop Reliability Trial. This took five days over rugged bush tracks. He served as a correspondent during the Boer War (he wanted to be a soldier but a withered arm determined that he go as a writer) and the Boxer Rebellion in China; then as a remount officer in the First World War, achieving the rank of major. He also became the editor of various Sydney journals. Having turned from the law to a successful writing career, he observed that he was making more money writing than he had ever made in the law.

Two years before his death in 1941, Andrew Barton Paterson was created a Commander of the Order of the British Empire (CBE).

Norman Lindsay

Few artists are more deserving of the epithets 'genius' and 'prolific' than Norman Lindsay. He was fortunate in being born into an artistic family. One of ten children, his siblings Percival, Lionel, Ruby and Daryl became well-known artists. The young Lindsays loved to dress up as Bacchanals and pose for classical orgy photographs, which no doubt influenced Norman's subject matter later in his career.

Mrs. Bush Pub (to travelling artist):
An' 'ow many o' these pictors can I 'ave for a shilling?
Artist: *That depends, madam, on how many weeks board and lodging I can have for a shilling.*
– The Bulletin, 1913

It is for his erotic nude-figure drawings, woodcuts, etchings, watercolours and oil paintings that he is most famous. Not surprisingly, these unashamed subjects were the target of many conservative critics and wowsers, with occasional censorship affecting the showing of his works. Even though attitudes are more liberal today, his subjects are still seen as risque. But given that he thought life should include some excitement and that the human figure was both beautiful and the most difficult subject to capture well, his art should not be simply dismissed by unappreciative non-art-lovers. He also enjoyed sculpture, writing, landscape

gardening and building model boats. Generations of Australian children have grown up with the delightful picture book, *The Magic Pudding*, which he wrote and illustrated.

When Norman was 17, he left his homctown of Creswick and joined his brother Lionel Lindsay in Melbourne. There, he roamed the streets, observing everyday life. He would wander through the morgue, courts, brothels, pubs, Chinese establishments in Little Bourke Street, theatres and prize-fights at the Stadium to find material for his drawings for *The Hawklet*, whose editor lived in a brothel.

A friend insisted on taking a couple of his drawings to show the editor of *The Bulletin*. 'By return post, I got a cheque for five pounds and was staggered in all my being for such a regal reward for two very inadequate pen drawings,' said Norman. So he moved to Sydney, and most of his comical art was drawn over a 50-year period for *The Bulletin*, the journal to which Banjo Paterson and Henry

Landscape artist: *I say, did you happen to see a lost dog?*
Inhabitant: *Wot sorter dorg?*
L.A.: *What sort! Oh, an awfully well-coloured dog – a raw sienna colour, you know, with a touch of orange in the highlights and burnt umber in the shadows.*
– The Bulletin, 1912

Lindsay had many devotees including Dame Nellie Melba. However, his paintings caused a great deal of public controversy. In 1931, Lindsay left for America saying, 'I'm sick and tired of this wowseristic country,' but he returned later and set about working again with great vigour. A year before Norman's death in 1969, Godfrey Blunden wrote, 'A generation has arrived which happily seeks out Norman Lindsay ... because in our drab and dangerous march to nowhere he is that rare, wonderfully reassuring and luminous event, a genius: perhaps the only authentic genius Australia has ever had.'

On the eve of his 90th birthday, Norman Lindsay published a book of pen drawings about which a Sydney critic wrote, 'They speak with the voice of an exuberant young man in the springtime; a man who has an unfading love affair with life.' Lindsay died a few months later.

Mulga Joe: Look at that artis' cove painting that blamed 'ole tumble-down 'umpy and taking no notice o' Ryan's grand new pub!
– The Bulletin, 1913

Lawson contributed so much. He made more than 10,000 drawings for *The Bulletin* and its sister magazine *The Lone Hand*. Many of the character types he drew were swagmen and bush folk.

Most pen drawings were made during a relatively short period of history – between the centuries of traditional woodcuts and the introduction of photo etching for letterpress printing using dot screens. Norman Lindsay was a fan of the great English art nouveau artist Aubrey Beardsley, who died at age 26. Another artist Lindsay admired was the Spaniard Daniel Vierge who, he said, was one of the greatest pen and ink draughtsmen. At the height of Vierge's career, his right arm became paralysed. Lindsay wrote, 'No worse evil could befall an artist – the spectre of a crippled right hand has haunted me all through life.'

The movie *Sirens*, starring Sam Neill, Elle MacPherson, Kate Fisher and Portia de Rossi, portrayed part of Lindsay's later life in the Blue Mountains, west of Sydney.

The story behind the song

The inspiration for 'Waltzing Matilda' was an event that brought Australia perhaps as close as it has been to civil war. In those days, the country's fortunes rose and fell with the price and demand for wool, with exports going to mills in the USA, Europe and the United Kingdom. 'Australia rides on the sheep's back' was a popular truism. With increasing demand for wool by British mills, the number of sheep in Australia rose from 21 million in 1861 to 107 million in 1891.

The Great Shearers' Strike took place in 1891 and was followed by a two-year phase of nervous peace that included occasional 'acts of incendiarism' – including the torching of several shearing-sheds. Winton in central Queensland was under martial law.

With the depression causing increased unemployment, many of those in work were forced to take pay cuts. With the ongoing drought and the introduction of the new, faster shearing machines replacing hand shears, it was inevitable that the Pastoralists' Association would want the pay cuts to extend to the shearers. But the shearers' union disagreed, and the 1894 shearers' strike spread throughout Queensland and New South Wales to parts of Victoria and South Australia.

A union leader roused the discontent to fever pitch by declaring that '10,000 bushmen behind 10,000 steel blades were the only remedy' for their grievances. A mock trial was held. 'The court' condemned the Queensland premier and local member to death and their effigies were set alight. Unionists visited woolsheds telling the shearers to clear out by sundown or receive a bullet in the backside. Eastern Australia had 3000 woolsheds, of which only 400 were not union sheds. Unionists dunked non-unionists in water-tanks. The government sent militia to escort non-union labour into the sheds.

Troubles peaked in western Queensland. To assist police and militia, civilians were enlisted as special constables in an attempt to subdue the well-organised, striking unionists. In Barcaldine alone, more than 1500 troopers with cannon and gattling guns fought to prevent 1000 armed shearers attacking a train loaded with non-union labourers. More than 800 shearers were arrested and 20 were subsequently sentenced to seven years' hard labour.

While steaming up the Darling River in 1894, the 106-foot (32 metre) paddle-steamer Rodney *was burned to the waterline then scuttled. She had more than 40 non-unionist labourers aboard and had stopped to refuel at a woodpile, then moored for the night near a swamp 'to be safe'. Next morning, she was boarded by masked men, who forced all personnel ashore then torched the vessel. Other vessels were pelted with whole and broken bottles.*

Shearing the Rams, 1890
Tom Roberts, born in Great Britain 1856, arrived in Australia 1869, died in 1931
Oil on canvas on composition board, 122.4 x 183.3 cm
Felton Bequest, 1932
National Gallery of Victoria, Melbourne

Completed in 1890, over two four-month shearing seasons, Roberts made 70 to 80 sketches for this magnificent painting in the shearing shed at Brocklesby station near Corowa, NSW, on the banks of the Murray River. He then returned to paint it in his studio.

Violence escalated. With roads being rocky and boggy, most were usable only by bullock dray, camel, bicycle or 'shank's pony' – slang for walking. So, shallow-draft paddle-steamers on the Murray, Darling and Murrumbidgee rivers were the principal means for transporting workers, supplies and police squads up-river – and wool down-river. The PS *Rodney* was transporting 'black legs' or 'scabs' (the unions' derisive terms for non-unionist labourers, who were in plentiful supply in those times of high unemployment) to the shearing-shed at Tolarno station, when a union mob raided it. They tossed the crew and passengers off the steamer. Then they doused the vessel with kerosene and burnt it to the waterline. The arsonists were never caught.

Billy McLean, a young shearer, was shot as he came to work at Grassmere station, just for entering a shearing-shed to talk to the non-union shearers. He was charged with unlawful assembly and sentenced to three years in gaol. He later died from the gunshot wounds to his lung.

At Oondooroo station a unionist attacked a volunteer worker and police and the station owners drove back the union mob. But next day armed strikers burned down the Ayrshire Downs woolshed. A state of emergency was declared, police were sent, including 80 specially sworn-in constables. Two unionists were shot. Nevertheless, thirteen woolsheds in this part of central Queensland were burnt down. The unionists moved from woolshed to woolshed on diverse routes, laying false trails. One record states that the military performed 'arduous marches ... 109 miles in 32 hours through flooded country, having to swim rivers'. Army privates earned the high rate for the time of six shillings a day.

The last property in Queensland to be attacked was Dagworth station at Kyuna. There was a violent gun battle and when the unionists burnt down the woolshed, 140 lambs

were incinerated along with many bales of wool. Following this, an old union organiser of German descent, Samuel 'Frenchy' Hoffmeister, returned to the union camp at the Four Mile Billabong beside the Diamantina River, six kilometres from Kyuna and committed suicide by shooting himself. We don't know exactly where this occurred. According to one theory, Hoffmeister died at Combo Waterhole, which is adjacent to the Diamantina River and twelve kilometres south of Kyuna off the Landsborough Highway.

A stockade was erected around another shed at Dagworth to be used by non-union shearers. Eventually the strike was called off, but the experience left the union shearers with lingering resentment towards the pastoralists. The strike contributed to the formation of the Australian Labor Party.

Enter Andrew Barton Paterson

The most widely accepted version of how 'Waltzing Matilda came to be written is as follows. In 1895 'The Banjo', who was 31 and still working as a solicitor, accompanied his fiancée of eight years, Sarah Riley, to Queensland to visit her brother at Vindex station near Winton. While there, they also visited the brothers of Sarah's school friend Christina MacPherson, whose family owned nearby Dagworth station – the last property to have been attacked in the shearers' strike.

14

Robert McPherson showed Paterson around and shared many bush stories with him. He taught Paterson much 'bush slanguage', discussed the shearers' strike and problems with the union, and related the story of Hoffmeister's suicide at the waterhole after the burning of the Dagworth woolshed. He told Paterson how he and a police constable had found the shearer's body with its self-inflicted bullet wound.

On another occasion McPherson showed him a partly-eaten wether (castrated male sheep) and told Paterson how a squatter, trooper and an Aboriginal tracker had come across a swagman, a wool scourer named George Pope, who had killed it. When the incriminating carcass was found, Pope threw himself into the waterhole to escape being charged, and drowned. This story, the term 'waltzing Matilda' and other bush slang took Banjo's fancy.

Years before, Sarah's school friend Christina MacPherson had heard a march from the Scottish song 'Thou Bonnie Wood of Craigielea' at the Warrnambool races, and she played it for the young couple on her zither. The tune was somewhat different to the one we know today. However, Banjo took to it and, using some of his newly learned bush lingo, penned words to go with it. His original lyrics were also a little different to today's version. The group performed it at the North Gregory Hotel and the song's fame began. It seems Banjo not only liked the Craigielea tune but Christina too. At any rate, when he and Sarah left Winton, they were no longer engaged.

In 1903, the song was used to advertise 'Billy Tea' and the business owner's wife, Marie Cowan, made minor changes to Paterson's words. She also played around with the tune and arrangement so much that only portions of the original can be recognised.

During the 1915 Gallipoli campaign the song gained popularity with the Anzac troops and has been a favourite with Australians young and old ever since. It is also recognised around the world as Australia's song.

You'll come a-waltzing Matilda with me!

Swagmen

'Swaggies' – more formally termed 'itinerant workers' – roamed the country looking for work during hard times. They camped out in the bush or, if they were lucky, would sleep in a shed on a farm and do odd jobs in return for meals.

A source for the distant background of this illustration was an oil painting by Penleigh Boyd from 1913, entitled *The Federal Capital Site*. The work is part of the Parliament House art collection in Canberra. Today, to the left of and beyond where the church still stands, is Lake Burley Griffin, named after the city's designer. The church (built in 1841) is the St John the Baptist Church & Schoolhouse Museum in Constitution Avenue.

In the early days, mileposts showed how many miles it was to the next town.

JIM (in the background): *'Yes, 'e's a clever feller, Bill is. There ain't no flies on him.'*
– The Bulletin, 1910

16

Once a jolly swagman

Rabbits   *Large egret*   *Galahs*   *Kookaburra (Laughing jackass)*

camped by a billabong,

Kangaroos   Kangaroo and joey

Billabong

When floods cause a meandering river to jump its banks and cut a corner, the cut-off bend in the river forms a 'billabong' – a separate small lake, usually an arc or horseshoe shape. These are usually attractive to the eye as water lilies grow in their still waters, and they teem with wildlife.

'I've boiled yer billy for yer.
Where's yer tea and sugar?'
'Wot! Ain't yer got none?'

19

Rabbits

20

White-faced heron   *Kangaroos*

under the shade

of a coolibah tree

Coolibah tree

Eucalyptus microtheca. Also known as coolybah, coolibar, dwarf box, coolabah, callaille, yathoo, targoon, western coolabah, narrow-leaved box or jimbul kurleah. Bark is rough on the trunk with smooth branches higher up. Apart from the tree that our jolly swagman camped under, Australia's most famous coolibah tree is perhaps the 'Dig Tree' on Cooper Creek at the site of the Burke and Wills Expedition Depot Camp 65, on which was inscribed 'B LXV DIG 3FT NW DEC 6, 60 – APR 21,61'. Food was buried by the leaving party. Burke and Wills arrived that evening but, due to a series of bungles, both perished some weeks later at the tree site.

PARSON: *'Don't go into that low place, my friend.'*
SWAGMAN: *All right, mate! I'm a stranger here! What pub d'you recommend?'*

21

22

And he sang as he watched

and waited till his billy boiled,

Billies and damper

After his swag, the next most important item in the swaggie's kit was his billy, followed by his pocket-knife and matches. His tin billy boiled water for his tea (he'd most likely never heard of a cappuccino!), roasted rabbit, poached poached lamb and boiled 'borrowed' vegetables. Overnight, underground cooking of rabbit in ashes was a delicious treat. Two traditions for billy tea are to put a gum leaf in with the water for an extra tang, and to spin the billy in an overarm action to aid the cooling of the tea. The billy was also waterproof storage for food, and for dry grass with which to start the next campfire. Damper is easy 'bush bread'. The basic recipe is simply flour and water combined into a dough and covered with ashes in the campfire. It's improved if you add a little salt, use self-raising flour and/or a little baking powder. It is also better if you use warm milk instead of water.

Damper may be cooked in a camp oven with ashes underneath and over it.

To test if it's cooked, tap the crust and it should sound hollow. Eat while it's hot with lashings of butter and honey.

NEW ARRIVAL: 'Well, there's one thing I like about this place, anyhow; a bloke can always light his pipe an' boil his billy nice and comfortable.'

'You'll come a-waltzing Matilda with me!'

Waltzing Matilda, waltzing Matilda, You'll come a-waltzing Matilda with me. And he

sang as he watched and waited till his billy boiled. You'll come a-waltzing Matilda with me.

Waltzing Matilda

While our swaggie has pinned his dream girl's photograph to his swag, she's not Matilda. It's his swag that is 'Matilda'.

'Waltzing Matilda' is sung in schools, on picnics, around the campfire and at parties. Almost everyone knows the words. It's sung to kick off Australian Rules football finals and all manner of other special events. It's sung without accompaniment, with lone guitars and by symphony orchestras with various arrangements. It was featured in the Opening Ceremony of the Sydney 2000 Olympic Games, which started with a stirring team of galloping high country horsemen in the style of 'The Man from Snowy River'.

'Waltzing Matilda' is our song.

SWAGGIE: *'Any work in the town back there, mate?*
TRAMP: *'Too blessed much work! Why, after I'd whitewashed the bloomin' cells an' cleaned up the yard, the blessed cops gets in a load o' wood.'*

Jumbuck: a sheep, an adaptation of an Aboriginal word for 'white mist'.

Down

to drink

Emus

Kangaroo

came a jumbuck

at that billabong.

LITTLE PAT PLUNKET: 'Hav' yez got a job ov wurrk yez e'd give to a mahn?'
COCKIE: 'Well, I dunno. Can yer milk?'
PAT: 'Milk, is it? Sure 'tis the first thing I iver did in me loife.'
– The Bulletin, 1909.

27

Up jumped the swagman

and grabbed him with glee.

PICNICKER: 'Would you mind lending us your billy to get a drink of water? It's clean, I suppose?'
SWAGGIE: 'My oath! I just biled some clothes in it.'
– The Bulletin, 1911.

And he sang as he shoved

that jumbuck in his tucker bag

FIRST SWAGGIE: *'Dash it, Bill. I've lost me knife. There's a hole in me pocket.'*
SECOND SWAGGIE: *'Ye must a' bin carryin' yer sovrins in it: they wears a pocket out quicker than anything.'*
(Sovereigns were gold coins used between 1855 and 1931, worth one pound.)

'You'll come a-waltzing Matilda with me!'

Tucker bag

A bag in which food is kept.
Swaggies often had a
separate bag or two and
sometimes they rolled
everything up in their swags.

Up rode the squatter,

mounted on his thoroughbred.

Kangaroos

Squatter

In 1831, the Colonial Office in London ordered that settlement should be limited to a tight semicircle around Sydney, but enterprising 'squatters' took their herds of sheep and cattle into the bush. Governor Bourke wrote that 'Not all the armies in England could drive them back.' He attempted to impose a levy on each beast but failed. The 1840–43 depression ruined many squatters but the survivors thrived, built great wealth and became the 'squattocracy' (landed gentry) of Australia. Later, land was handed out to soldier-settlers and others, but the best land had gone.

MANAGER (to applicant for job): 'Can you ride?'
MYALL JOE: 'My oath. I was born in the saddle.'
MANAGER: 'Oh, you were, were you?'
MYALL JOE: 'Fact, boss. The old people was ridin' into Bourke to see the doctor.'
– *The Bulletin*, 5 October 1911

Down came

Troopers

Mounted Police were not in sufficient numbers during the shearers' strike of 1894, so many specially sworn-in constables were appointed and the military was called in. Thousands of troopers were spread out over the eastern states – sometimes well over 1000 in one small area. The unmounted police undertook long and arduous marches, and sometimes had to cross rivers to take their prisoners to lockups.

the troopers one, two, three.

'I'm wet to the skin.'
'So'm I. But I wouldn't moind THAT if I wasn't
so bloomin' dry.'
– The Bulletin, 1915

'Whose that jolly jumbuck

Crime and punishment

In periods of social unrest, crimes against property attracted heavy punishment. Capital punishment by hanging was still in force. Even 'jumping the rattler' (catching a goods train illegally, which was a common practice with swagmen) meant a gaol sentence. So to be caught stealing and eating a sheep often meant severe punishment.

'Want a job?'
'Gotter job.'
'What sorter job?'
'Lookin' for a job.'
– The Bulletin, 1918

you've got in your tuckerbag?

You'll come a-waltzing
Matilda with me!'

Up jumped the swagman,

sprang into the billabong.

'I don't hold with carryin' a lookin'-glass.
They make yer face look so dirty.'
– The Bulletin, 1932

'You'll never catch me

alive!' said he.

SWAGGIE: 'Any chance of a bit of meat, boss?'
COCKY: 'Well, I can't spare any meat, but I'm going to kill a pumpkin tonight, an' you can have the innards!'

And his ghost may be heard
as you pass by that billabong,

Large egret

'I got a beer at my last house. How did you get on?'
'Rotten. They gimme a suit of clothes.'
– The Bulletin, 1933

43

'You'll come a-waltzing
Matilda with me.'

The Southern Cross

At the time of the 1894 shearers' strike, the Union Jack was still flown all over Australia. After competitions and refinements, our current flag featuring the Southern Cross was approved in 1903.

'I can understand, Moike, how they measure the distance of thim starrs and weigh them, but what bothers me is how they foind out their names.'
– The Bulletin, 1902

Above is the original music score by Christina Macpherson made in 1895. It shows Banjo Paterson's original wording, in Christina's handwriting. It was Christina who left the only documentation about the origin of 'Waltzing Matilda', when she wrote in a letter: 'On this occasion my brother & Mr. Patterson [sic] were out riding & they came to a waterhole (or billabong) & found the skin of a newly killed sheep – all that was left by a swagman – and he made use of this incident.'

Christina had heard the old Scottish tune 'Thou Bonnie Wood of Craigielea' years before at the races in Warrnambool, Victoria, so it is possible that when she played it on her zither, even this version did not exactly match the original. If you are a musician and play this music, you will find that only a portion of it is familiar when matched with today's version.

In 1903, Marie Cowan rearranged the words and the music to promote her husband's brand of 'Billy Tea'. Today's popular song is shown on the opposite page.

Banjo's original words were:

Oh! There once was a swagman camped in a Billabong,
 Under the shade of a Coolabah tree;
And he sang as he looked at his old billy boiling,
 'Who'll come a-waltzing Matilda with me?'

(Chorus:) Who'll come a-waltzing Matilda, my darling,
 Who'll come a-waltzing with me?
Waltzing Matilda and leading a water-bag –
 Who'll come a-waltzing Matilda with me?

Down came a jumbuck to drink at the water-hole,
 Up jumped the swagman and grabbed him with glee;
And he sang as he stowed him away in his tucker-bag,
 'You'll come a-waltzing Matilda with me!'

Down came the Squatter a-riding his thoroughbred;
 Down came Policemen – one, two and three.
'Whose is the jumbuck you've got in the tucker-bag?
 You'll come a-waltzing Matilda with me.'

But the swagman, he up and he jumped in the waterhole,
 Drowning himself by the Coolabah tree;
And his ghost may be heard as it sings in the Billabong,
 'Who'll come a-waltzing Matilda with me?'

Even though Banjo was staying at the Macpherson station with his fiancée Sarah Riley, he and Christina became close enough for the engagement to be broken. Were the words *'Who'll come a-waltzing, my darling ... with me?'* the first daring approach Banjo made to Christina? Whether the song started with a romance or not, it has certainly created a great romance between Australians and the song 'Waltzing Matilda'.

46

Waltzing Matilda

A.B. PATERSON

MARIE COWAN

1. Once a jol - ly swag - man_ camp'd_ by a bil - la - bong
2. Down came a jum - buck_ to drink at that bil - la - bong
3. Up___ rode the squat - ter_ mount - ed on his thor - ough - bred
4. Up___ jump'd the swag - man_ sprang in - to the bil - la - bong

Un - der the shade of a cool - i - bah__ tree And he sang as he watch'd and
Up jumped the swag-man_ and grabbed him with glee And he sang as he shoved that
Down came the troop-ers__ One__ Two__ Three Whose that jol-ly jum-buck you've
"You'll nev - er catch me__ a - - live" said he And his ghost may be heard as you

wait - ed till his bil - ly boil'd
jum-buck in his tuck- er bag
got in your__ tuck-er bag
pass by that__ bil - la - bong

You'll come a waltz - ing Ma - til - da with me

Waltz-ing Matil-da Waltz-ing Matil-da You'll come a waltz-ing Ma-til-da with me.

And he
And he
Whose that
And his

sang as he watch'd and wait-ed til his bil - ly boil'd
sang as he shoved that jum-buck in his tuck-er bag
jol - ly jum-buck you've got__ in your tuck-er bag
ghost may be heard as you pass_ by that bil-la-bong

"You'll come a waltzing Ma-til-da with me."

47

Being Australian

G'day. Mateship. A fair go.
These terms are unique to Australia and go a long way to explaining the Australian psyche. People around the world are familiar with the friendly 'G'day' greeting offered to all and sundry, providing they look friendly or could be stirred into looking friendly. Australians have cultivated a society that is less stratified than most.

A large Australian company recently conducted research to assess its staff's motivations. The results showed that, more than money, security or pride, the opportunity to help their mates was their strongest motivating force at work.

We live in a country where vast numbers of volunteers helped out at the Sydney 2000 Olympic Games, and every day volunteers help large numbers of charities to help others. That's mateship. Our collective Australian personality values honesty, morality, fairness, opportunity and just plain decency.

Beginning with the Aboriginal peoples, who first arrived many thousands of years ago, we are all immigrants to this great land. Our national anthem, 'Advance Australia Fair' states that we are young and free. That gives us a good start in 'having a go' and 'giving our mates a fair go'. We now have people from well over a hundred countries living together in what is one of the most successful multicultural countries in the world.

Samuel Hoffmeister, one of the figures on whom Banjo Paterson's song 'Waltzing Matilda' was based was a recent immigrant. But the swagman in the song is not one man. He is a composite figure, the epitome of 'the little Aussie battler'.

If you're a recent immigrant to Australia, welcome to this great country of ours. You'll soon understand the meaning of 'We are one. We are many. I am, you are, we are Australian' and 'I still call Australia home'.

Boil a billy, share some damper, throw some prawns on the barbie, sing 'Waltzing Matilda' and 'sing with one voice'.

G'day, mate!